I0164716

Children Think Suicide, Too!

LESLIE A. HILL

Copyright ©2014 Leslie A. Hill

All rights reserved. Except for brief excerpts for review
purposes, no part of this book may be reproduced or used in
any form without written permission from the publisher.

All scripture quotations, unless otherwise noted, are taken
from the Holy Bible, New King James Version (KJV), English
Standard Version (ESV) and the New American Standard Bible
(NASB) Version. All versions of the Holy Bible are from
Youversion.com.

Cover: Canva.com
Photo Credit: Jermaine Manor
Published by Royal Court Books.

Printed in the United States of America
First edition 2015

ISBN:978-0-9856929-1-9

Dedication

In loving memory of Myrtle Elizabeth Hill, my mom, who loved and raised me to the best of her ability as a single parent. Mr. Sterling, my God father who was my inspiration and friend. You showed me love from a father's perspective, even though you had no children of your own. My neighbors, Mrs. Mary and Mr. Fred and their English bulldog, Spot. You both watched over me every day before and after school. My Aunt Florence, my mother's oldest sister, also known to me as Aunt Sister, you were my guiding light in showing me what love is all about in so many ways. You literally saved my life.

Although you all are not with me today, your spiritual presence will be with me until the day it is time for me to join you in heavenly bliss. I love and miss you all.

INTRODUCTION

This book was also written for all children who have lost their lives to suicide. To the parents who could not or just did not see the signs of depression that preceded it. To the friends and relatives who suffer the loss of that loved one; and to those who do not realize, the lack of love can have a profound effect on a child's psyche.

This book was not written to prevent suicide but to let you be aware of some of the signs I went through as a child and a teen. Lastly, to let you all know that suicide is a permanent end to existence. It doesn't have to be that way if you just know the signs, get your child the professional help he or she needs, and to love them as God loves you. God expects you to be the best parent you can be accepting the good, the bad and the ugly but he also expects you to turn to him in all your needs.

"Teaching them to observe all things whatsoever I have commanded you: and, lo, I am with you always, even unto the end of the world, Amen." (Matthew 28:20 KJV)

WHAT DOES SUICIDE MEAN?

Suicide – "is to some it's just a word in the dictionary; to others it's a broken heart from the loss of a loved one who took their life." To God, it's a great sadness and breaks the His heart. To the enemy, Satan, it's a wonderful thing because he wants to control of your life and will try to convince you take your own life.

The bible says he is out to rob, steal and kill anything or anyone important to God. He will try to trick you just as he did in the garden with Adam and Eve. Jesus came later so that we have life more abundantly.

"The thief comes only to steal and kill and destroy; I have come that they may have life, and have it to the fullest." (John 10:10 NASB)

Definition: suicide - su-i-cide /

1.   Noun – The action of killing oneself intentionally; "he committed suicide at the age of forty".

2.   Verb – Intentionally killing ones' self.

Synonyms - self-destruction, or self-murder; take one's own life; Make away with ones' self.

WHAT DOES GOD SAY ABOUT SUICIDE?

"Be not overly wicked, neither be a fool. Why should you die before time" (Ecclesiastes 7:17 ESV)

"You shall not murder." (Exodus 20:13 ESV)

"If anyone destroys God's temple, God will destroy him. For Gods' temple is holy, and you are that temple."

(I Corinthian 3:17 ESV)

"Or do you not know that your body is a temple of the Holy Spirit within you, whom you have from God? You are not your own, for you were bought with a price. So glorify God in your body." (I Corinthians 6:19 -20 ESV)

"Do you not know that you are God's temple and that Gods Spirit dwells in you"? (I Corinthian 3:16 ESV)

"So God created man in his own image, in the image of God he created him: male and female he created them." (Genesis 1:27 ESV)

"For you formed my inward parts; you knitted me together in my mother's womb. I praise you, for I am fearfully and wonderfully made." Wonderful are your works; my soul knows it very well." (Psalm 139:13-17 ESV)

You see your life is important to God – life is the most precious gift in the world. We were given life to praise and glorify God; it is not ours to take; no matter what type of life you're living or what has happened to you. You must constantly give all your woes and sorrows to him and praise him in good and bad times.

WHAT DO PARENTS THINK?

Many parents think that suicide will never happen to their child(ren). I believe that everyone in their lifetime thinks about it; children think about it in ways that cannot be expressed as an adult might express it. By the time you realized that your child is thinking about it, it is maybe too late; they may have attempted it, or committed it and have passed away.

Usually when children do not want to be in a particular home or uncomfortable situation and are pushed to the brink where they feel like dying, it is very overwhelming mentally and they just don't know how to do it. By the time a child is between the ages of 10 – 12 years old, they start to become creative in handling their frustration, disappointments and sadness and begin to search for ways to end their life. Some children act out and the acting out continues to grow into a destructive manner, if there is no intervention.

In my life time, I have seen suicidal attempt's proceeded itself by depression, the destruction that comes in many forms such as: abuse of self, abuse of others, verbal abuse, abuse of animals, overeating, starving yourself, continual tantrums, failing grades, an obsession with death or dead things, withdrawing for others, crying all the time, drinking, drugs, self-mutilation and bullying are just a few.

As a young student I found several reference of information in library books on suicide. I thought well if it's in a book it could possibly happen and maybe I could do it right. I was surprised to find information so accessible.

I believe a person is not crazy to want to commit suicide but has an over whelming feeling of not wanting to be here on this earth or not be in a particular upsetting or devastating situation. Truly they want to go someplace better as I will explain in my story.

MY STORY

I can remember as far back as four or five years old. As a young girl, I was looking for love from my mom as all children do. I was raised without my father being present so I did not know the love of an earthly father. However, I did have the love of a heavenly father, and my Godfather, Mr. Sterling. He was the greatest Godfather a child could ever have. He read me stories; made me lunch, bought me a bike for my birthday and taught me how to ride it with confidence. He bought me Barbie dolls, and even made me a black baby doll out of corn husk like his mom did, when he was a child. He would tell me all kind of kid jokes, which always make me laugh. He would watch me when my mom had to go to work, or when I was sick, and would pamper me the whole time. Through all that love, I still felt something was missing at home.

My mom was saddened by the relationship with my biological dad, whom I did not know. She never told me anything about him or where he lived. From what I could tell, they did not talk at all. My mom seemed a little distant and withdrawn at times never cuddling or hugging me as often as I needed. At bed time she gave me a quick hug and kiss on the forehead. That was ok then but as I grew older it felt empty. To me, she seemed sad all the time, so I would tell her the kid jokes my God father told me or try to do magic to make her laugh. Sometimes she laughed and sometimes she just smiled. Sometimes she seemed off at a distance.

I knew from going to church my mom was supposed to tell me she loved me and that Jesus loves me; because we sang that song "Jesus Loves Me Yes I Know" all the time. So I ran up to my mom after church and said, "hey mom guess what?" She said, "What!" with a big smile I said, "I love you, mommy." To my surprise, she was silent and gave me a halfcocked smile and said, "mmm hmm me too." I was very saddened because that was not the response I was looking for. That is not what I wanted to hear; I wanted her to hear her say, "I love you too" and give me a big hug and maybe a kiss on the cheek. I quietly accepted the smile and went with my friends. I was confused; wasn't she supposed to smile and say, "I love you too," and hug me? I wanted to ask my friends but I was afraid. When we went home, I was very quiet just trying to understand. As a 5-year-old, I did not know what to ask my mom, even though there were so many questions roaming around in my head. That night, I remember going to bed very sad.

When I went back to church the next week, I watched the parents dropping their children off in my class and randomly saying I love you, holding their children's hands, and hugging them. I thought, 'that's weird, I only held my mom's hand crossing the street. Why can't she hold my hand like that?' I asked myself, "why are their parents telling them they love them?", and mine just says, "me too." When I say I love you, mommy and she says me too, what does that mean?' So I went home again after church sad.

While playing with my dolls I got a burst of courage and said abruptly, "hey mommy, guess what, I love you, mommy" and all she said was, "yes you do". At that point, my heart was broken; it sunk to my feet. I became a sad depressed little girl. Even though my brother and sister lived with me, I felt lonely all the time. They were much older than me: my sister by 8 years and my brother by 12 years. They were not affectionate to me nor did I see them being affectionate with my mom. They barely played with me and when they did they would never let me win. My mom would play sometimes but not as much as I wanted her to.

The next week I asked my mom; "Do I have a daddy?" And she said, "of course you do." I asked, "Where is he?" and she said, "your dad is your heavenly father and that's all you need to know." That made me angry because I had questions. Was I adopted, left on this doorstep, am I really your child? I felt I was missing something so I prayed and asked God what I was supposed to do. I told him, I was very, very, very sad and asked him why my mom won't tell me she loves me like all the other kid's mom do. I wanted to know where my dad was and maybe he could tell me he loved me. As I prayed a peace came over my little tearful face and still kneeling in prayer, I fell asleep at my bedside.

The next morning, I asked my mom, "if I had a real dad and would he tell me, I love you?" My mom was surprised by the question, frowned and said harshly, "Why are you asking about a dad?" Before I could answer, she hurriedly changed the subject and said, "Let's get ready for school."

Even as a child, you know when someone is avoiding questions or ignoring you, so I just finished getting ready for school and said no more for that day.

As I began my walk to school, I should have been thinking about kindergarten, but my mind began to wonder. If my mom cannot tell me she loves me, or hugs me when I need it, does that make me a bad kid, or am I just unlovable?

"SPOT"

My neighbors, Ms. Mary and Mr. Fred, lived in the apartment above us. They had an English Boxer named Spot. I knew he loved me because he would greet me on the porch and try to follow me to school. He would lick my face even though I did not like doggy licks but I knew they were doggy kisses. They said Spot wags his tail and drools because he loves you and is happy to see you. I thought how could a simple dog express love and my mom can't? I began to ask, "Why does God love me and does not see me and my mom who sees me every day cannot say she loves me, even though she takes care of me every day?"

MY SIBLINGS

My sister, who was 13, did not like watching me would leave me every chance she got. My brother, who was 17 years old, used to kick me out his room and call me butthole but in a derogatory way. I came to the conclusion that none of them loved me but I knew God loves me and maybe I should just go and be with him. But how does a 5-year-old go to be with God and it's not her time? In reality, that was the beginning of disaster. I had let the enemy in with a single innocent suicidal thought. I wanted to die and go to heaven.

MY FIRST THOUGHTS

At night, my mom taught me a prayer: *Now I lay me down to sleep, I pray the lord my soul to keep, if I should die before I awake, I pray the lord my soul to take*. I changed the prayer to, *Now I lay me down to sleep, I pray the lord my soul to keep, let me die before I awake, I pray the lord my soul you can take.* Every day, I would wake up in tears because God had not come to take me with him. I wanted desperately to be in the arms of someone, anyone even if it meant dying. I wanted to be in heaven and be with the God I sang about. I wanted to die but did not know how to do it.

15

Who was going to expressed love me? How could I exist with no love in my own home? I would talk to my baby dolls and tell them *if* I grow up I am going to be a better mommy. I'd tell my kids I love them every day and hug them until they said let go. My thoughts of leaving this earth and being with my heavenly father was a *daily* thought. That is a lot for a child to think about.

THE THOUGHTS OF A YOUNG CHILD

The thought of suicide in a child lingers, once the thought is implanted in the mind, it will be there until it is explained to them, resolved or that child is delivered. Children do not understand it; they only know it as I do not want to be here anymore, I am not happy. Then a deep sadness sets in also known as childhood depression. Sometimes children become resourceful and will create an imaginary friend. I created an imaginary mother and dad when I played with my dolls and my tea set. Some children with traumatic situations may separate themselves and create other personalities.

All in all, it becomes more confusing each year you get older because most children will not tell anyone how they feel and most adults don't have a clue why their child is sad and don't ever take the time to ask the child how they feel. I guess you could say I lost the trust of my mother but I still loved her.

MY STORY PART 2

At around age 6, I had a party; my mom invited a few friends. I thought that was nice of my mom, maybe she loves me after all. So when I make a wish and blow out the candles I will wish for her to say "Happy Birthday, I love you!" Well, as you can imagine, that did not happen. All I got was "happy birthday" from everyone who was there and presents. I was grateful and should have been happy with that but I wasn't. I didn't even want the presents anymore; I wanted my mom to say I love you, and hug me and kiss me.

My God father said "I love you now open your presents." That moment meant the world to me, even though it came from him and not from her. He brought me a bike, it did not have training wheels, but it did have streamers and a horn. Temporarily, I was the happiest kid on the block.

MY AUNT SISTER

There were other small moments that made me happy, that was playing with my cousins and spending the night there. I got to spend the night after I turned 7 and boy did I have fun. There, I blended in amongst 7 children and grandchildren. When my Aunt

Florence aka Aunt Sister said, "I love you all," I knew that included me. I believe those are the words that saved me. She did stuff with us, cooked good food, let us do things for her and, in return, I got hugs and kisses. She would let Uncle Johnny take us for rides in his station wagon, to get goodies at the two local stores. I often wished she was my mom and he was my dad.

One day I asked Aunt Sister, "Do you think my mommy loves me? She said with a surprised look, "Why yes your mommy loves you; she just shows it to you instead of telling you. She just doesn't know how to say it". Aunt Sister told me, "when you bake cookies and cakes with your mom; she loves you, when she buys you pretty dresses and shoes, its love too, when she takes you to church it is definitely love. When she smiles at you she loves you more." Auntie Sister said "your mom is a doer, not a speaker".

She also told me I could come over whenever I wanted to and stay as long as I like. For some reason, that made sense to me and was very comforting.

With that coming from my aunt, I was somewhat satisfied and the thoughts of not wanting to be here on this earth slowly went away with each smile my mom gave me. My aunt told me to always tell your mommy you love her when the thought comes in my mind. She said maybe you can teach her too say it one day. So I did just that, told her I love her at random times and I would look at her to make sure she smiled at my gesture and she did smile every time even though she did not say anything.

That small piece of information my aunt had given me about my mother was a life saver for me, she cared about me and shared a piece of information about my mom I did not know and understand. She saw the pain in my eyes and the yearning in my heart, she knew it helped me to understand it was not me that was unlovable but my mom had issues expressing the love she had for me.

As a child, you think your parent can do no wrong or have any issues. I was the only child of my mom's three children who wanted to express love and now I was able to express love without expecting anything back. My aunt gave me the courage I needed to love myself no matter what other people thought, did or said to me. She told me I was born to love and let no one stop me from expressing it. She said you have a gift that no one else in the house has, and that is to love unconditionally. She called me "lovey dovey". I did not know what that meant but I knew it was a good thing. I now had a purpose that God gave only me and not by brother and sister. That night when I prayed, I asked God to forgive me for wanting to join him so soon and asked could I please let me stay her for a little while longer to be with my cousin's friends and my mom. Even though she would not tell me she loved me, I would tell her at least a couple times a week that I loved her, and I was happy with that.

MY SECOND THOUGHT

Once you have been exposed to a suicidal thought it may not be readily present at times but it does remain in your subconscious. The enemy will always be trying to bring the thought back because he wants your soul. My second thought of suicide happened at age 16, I was in a relationship that did not go well and a horrible thing happened to me. I came home and told my mom, what happened to me but she did not believe anything I told her. I was afraid to go to the hospital; I did not want anyone to judge me or say it was my fault.

My mom did not believe what had just happened and in a nasty tone, she asked, "Well, what did you do to provoke the incident?" I was crushed by that question. Wow, if she does not believe me then no one will. I walked away holding back the tears and crying as silent as I could in my room. As I lay in my bunk bed, I decided to call the hospital for some advice. They informed me to call the police and come to the hospital for an exam. I was so afraid to be interrogated by the police and doctors; I did not go to the police or the hospital.

I felt so unworthy, of being a female; unworthy of being God's little girl. I did however call my best friend and she asked "did you ask for it?" I told her the story and all she said was "was I'm glad it's not me and I hope you're not pregnant." I was mad at her for a long time for saying that, I wanted sympathy and comfort from her. My abuser told me if I went to the police he would kill me and hurt my mom. My first thought was go ahead and do it, you have ruined my life anyway but leave my mom alone. I also thought, my mom has not met you and she would not see it coming. I could not let my mom get hurt so I told no one else.

I got really depressed and withdrawn after that incident. I did not know what to do with all those emotions. My mind was free and roaming in the wrong direction and in came creeping that old thought of suicide again. With no one watching me or knowing how sad I was, I retreated to the bathroom, took a shower, and without any thought, downed a bottle of pills. I went to bed hoping I would fall into a deep sleep and not wake up in the morning. I felt now that all this is happened it would be best to end my life.

To my surprise, I woke up sick with a stomach ache. My mom had no idea what I had done the night before. She took me to the hospital and I just told them I took many pills in a small period of time. I did not want to be called crazy or sent to a psychiatric room. The way the nurse looked at me I don't think she believed me. That morning I totally shut down, I could not look my mother in the eye and our relationship changed over the next several years. I wanted her so badly to say I still love you, even though that happened to you. But she did not.

DELIVERANCE

About two years later, while attending my home church and watching Christian programming from time to time on channel 13, I heard a man say, "it's not your fault and God hears your cries, you are still as important to him now just as you were when you were a little girl and I do love you and can heal your broken heart and make you brand new. April 11, 1986, I went to church and gave my life back to Christ. I knew he would accept me as I am, clean me up and give me a new sense of being. That allowed me to love and express love again.

CONCLUSON

My main reason for writing this book is due to sadness I see when I hear tragic stories on TV or from people I to work "my son or daughter killed themselves; they were only 10 or 12 years old. I don't know what happened. I did not see the signs." It breaks my heart to hear something like this and I know it can be stopped; but only if we can be in tuned with our children. If we just pay attention to what a child needs and protect them the way God meant to be.

I have known several friends whose children have had bad experiences and experienced the thoughts of suicide. By sharing my experience at age 5-6 along with how God finally delivered me, I was able to help them get through it and get the help they needed. I am proud to say that through my experience, I am more in tune to children's expressions and how they feel. As a mother and caregiver of grandchildren, nieces, nephews, and a mentor to my friends' children, I believe I can pretty much read some of those sad faces and mental state of mind. That alerts me to at least ask them questions on how they feel and why they may be sad or withdrawn.

Children are basically vulnerable souls who need our help and guidance. I have seen children torn up by the Children and Youth Services with broken hearts from not being with their parents or grandparents. Some have even told me of situations of molestation and too embarrassed to tell their parents but they saw fit to tell me. When I look into a child's eyes and I see sadness, I have to know what's behind it; I want to know if I can help. You should want to know also. Look into your child eyes can you see the happiness or do you see the pain hidden behind them.

It is wonderful to tell a child that in spite of their situation that they are loved and needed. They are wonderfully created and loved by God. The smallest gesture of kindness and love can affect a child so they can see their worth. It should be our mission as a parent to get them to talk about whatever they are going through, and to listen without judging. Children are not meant to grow up to be depressed suicidal adults full of anxiety. No one wants to be alone, be picked on or feel unwanted or unloved. No one!!!

KNOW SOME SYMPTOMS

Symptoms in children can range from: imaginary friends, not wanting to go to school, crying for nothing when alone, isolation from family members or siblings, being mean to animals, siblings or other children, wanting to hurt themselves, not wanting to wake up, sudden sadness all the time (depression), and yes children get depressed too, they get very emotional, and children cry for any reason. Older children resort to drinking and wanting to take drugs to numb the pain. These symptoms I have listed are just some of which I know of and have experienced with myself, family and friends. They are not the only symptoms.

Begin to get in tuned to your child(ren), children of relatives', and children in your neighborhood. Show them that you love them, tell them that you love them and tell them you care what happens to them. Hug them. Talk to them. Conversation for children starts at age 2. They begin to understand more about how the world works. You must be their eyes and ears.

With everyone using multimedia now, your child sees more than his or her share of violence and negativity. If possible, don't let them watch violence on TV or play violent games. If you are going to let them play or watch violence, you should explain it to them. Children will act out everything they see and hear. If it is positive, then positive things will come out. If it is negative, then negative things will come out. Sometimes reality and make believe sometimes get intertwined and they do not know one from the other. Young children do not have the sense to know if it is real or fake. If they are having trouble at school, address it immediately or you will lose the trust of your child. All of these negative things affect our children; they are just that, children, not mini adults. Their level of understanding is not as great as an adult so don't treat them like one.

Nurturing is what they need. (Proverbs 22:6) NJV says, "Train up a child in the way he should go, and when he is old he will not depart form it". If you train them in violence, they will be violent. If you train your child in grace, they will be graceful. If you train your child in love, they will learn to love. I am glad my mom took me to church and now I know the saving power of our Lord and Savior, Jesus Christ.

LAST BUT EQUALLY IMPORTANT

Children are precious little beings. It is easy to overlook them assuming that they aren't old enough to do anything for the Lord. God can use anyone at any age, at any time however he chooses. He can use any one who is willing to yield to him. Jesus made it clear that children are important as in the story told in (Matt 18:2-6.) This story is to give you a sense of hope and to show you the importance God gives children.

www.ingramcontent.com/pod-product-compliance
Lightning Source LLC
Chambersburg PA
CBHW060549030426
42337CB00021B/4510